Fingerpower® Etudes

Level Two

Melodic Technic Studies
Compiled, edited and arranged by Wesley Schaum

Foreword

The purpose of these etudes is to offer technical experiences beyond the traditional Fingerpower® books. The etudes are more musical and melodic than standard exercises. The student develops technical prowess playing pieces that are both appealing and satisfying.

Level Two presents excerpts derived from eleven different master technic composers. The exercises are modified or transposed to achieve equal hand development and make them appropriate for this level. The pieces feature a planned variety of technical styles along with differing key signatures, time signatures and tempos.

The sources of the etudes are numerous concert pianists and teachers famous for their insights and development of successful piano technic, particularly during the 1800's. Students will benefit by exposure to the rich variety of this technic heritage.

The etudes are arranged in order of increasing difficulty. As the student advances, the progress in these pieces will complement the progress in a method book at the same level.

Practice Suggestions

To derive the most benefit from these etudes, attention should be given to how they are practiced. Careful listening is necessary to hear a good balance between the accompaniment and the melody. It is also important to listen for steady and accurate rhythm, and to make sure each finger plays equally loud, especially the 4th and 5th fingers.

Each assigned etude should be practiced four or five times daily, starting at a slow tempo and gradually increasing the speed as proficiency improves. Several previously learned etudes should be reviewed each week as part of regular practice. The printed metronome speeds are advisory and may be changed at the teacher's discretion.

EXCLUSIVELY DISTRIBUTED BY

HAL•LEONARD® CORPORATION
7777 W. BLUEMOUND RD. P.O. BOX 13819 MILWAUKEE, WI 53213

Composer Index • Level 2

6/8 Phrase Study

Johann H. Berens, Op. 70, No. 16

4

Legato Broken Chords

Cantabile ♩ = 132-144

Bernhard Wolff, Op. 130, No. 42

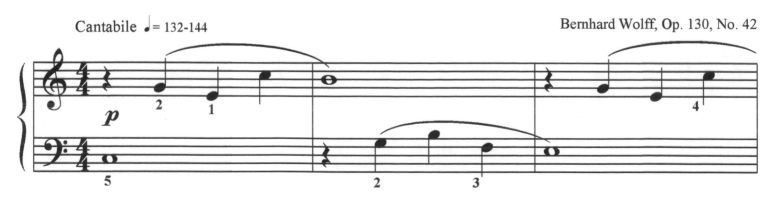

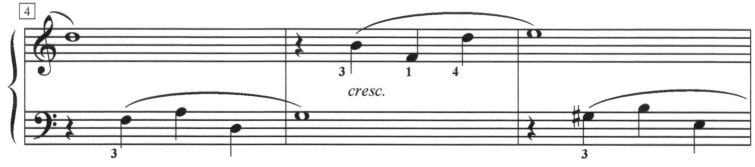

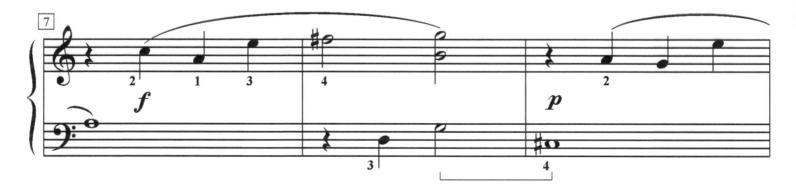

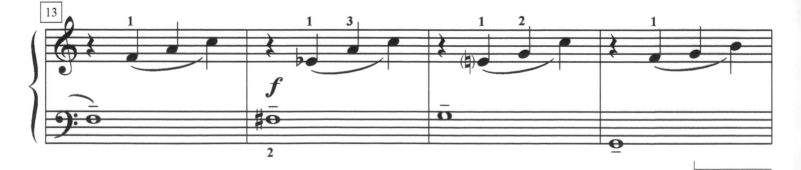

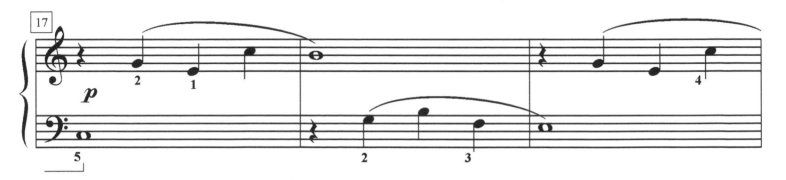

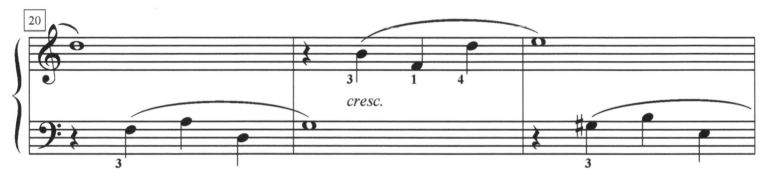

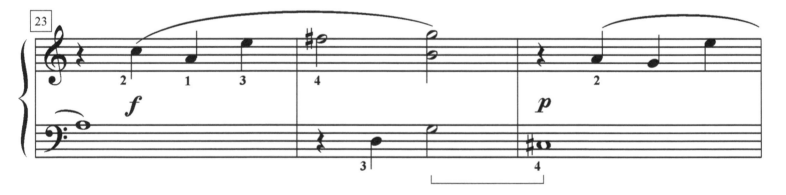

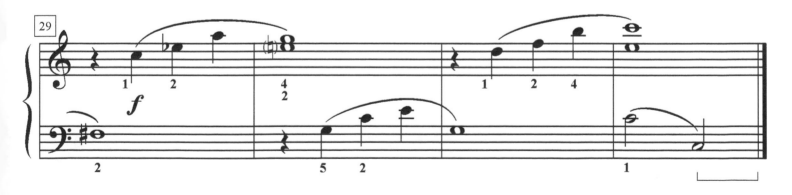

Scale Patterns

Louis Streabbog, Op. 63, No. 1

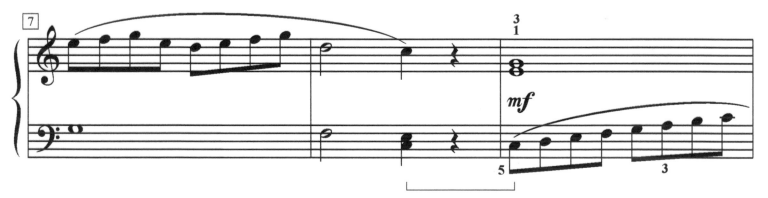

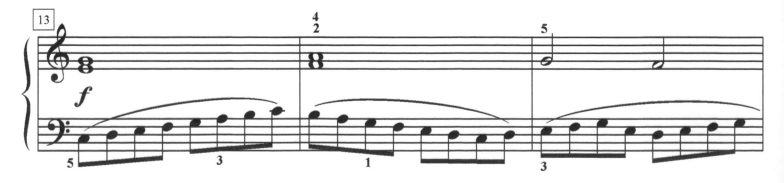

Legato Study

Larghetto ♩. = 56-60

Cornelius Gurlitt, Op. 82, No. 41

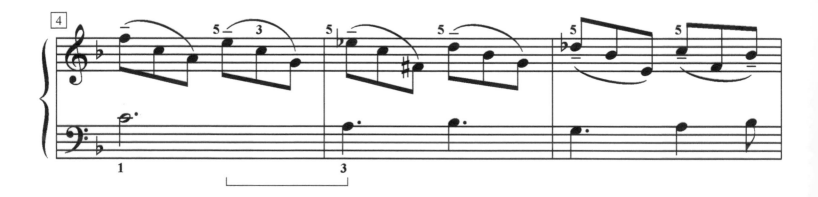

9

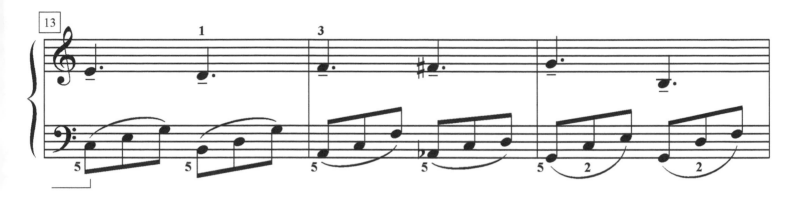

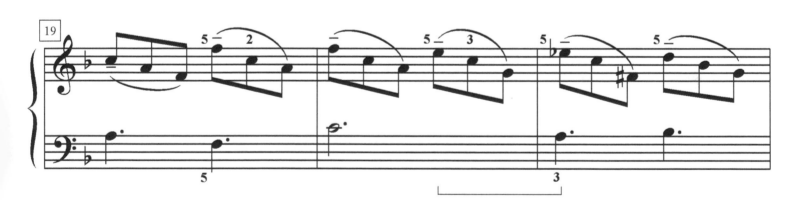

Five-Finger Drill

Andante ♩ = 76-84

Bernhard Wolff, Op. 130, No. 16

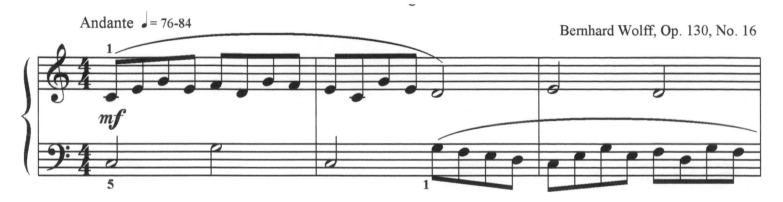

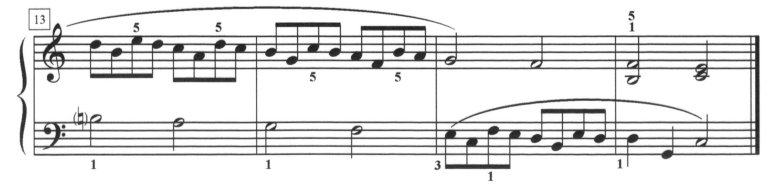

G-Major Patterns

Friedrich Brauer, Op. 15, No. 10

Andantino ♩ = 92-100

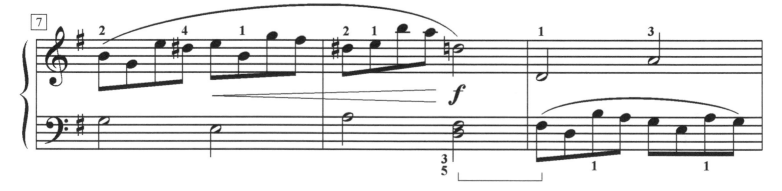

Broken Chord Etude

Cantabile ♩. = 60-66

Albert Biehl, Op. 44, No. 11

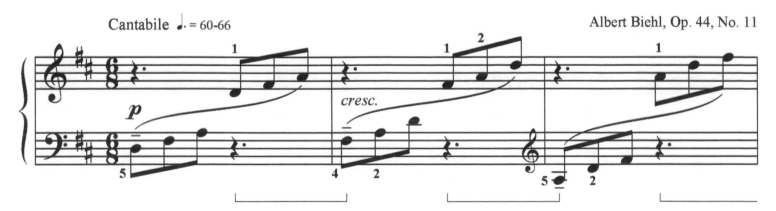

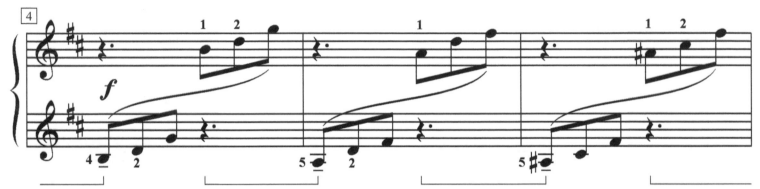

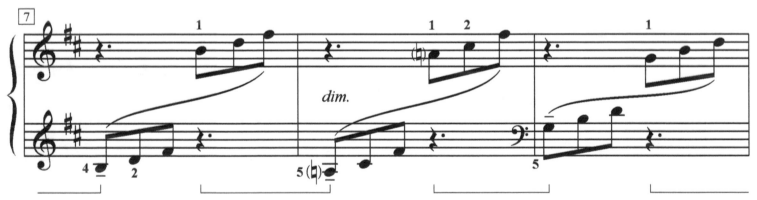

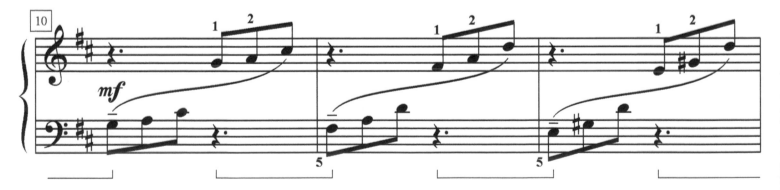

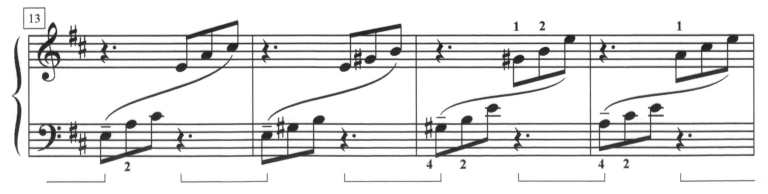

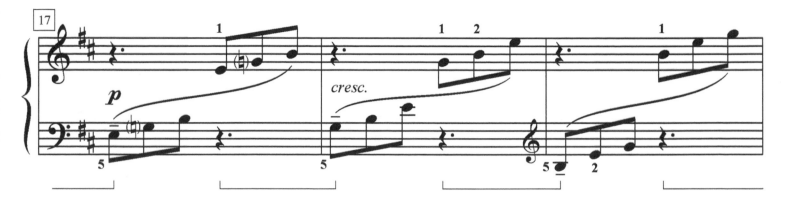

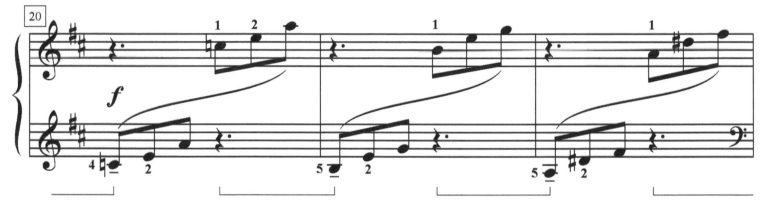

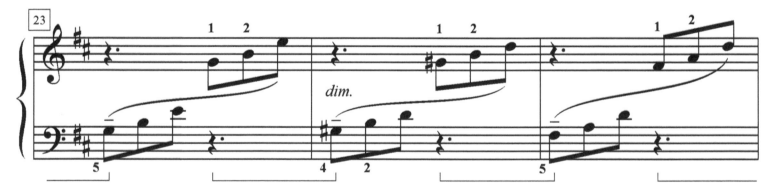

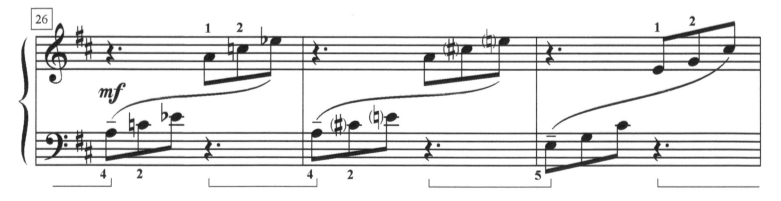

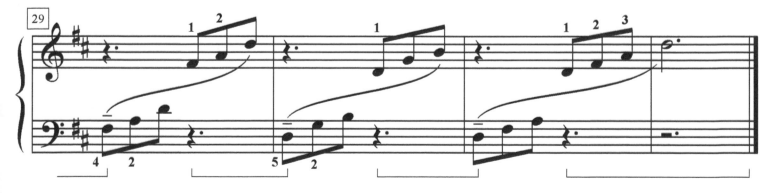

Hidden Melody

Giocoso ♩= 116-126

Ferdinand Beyer, Op. 101, No. 73

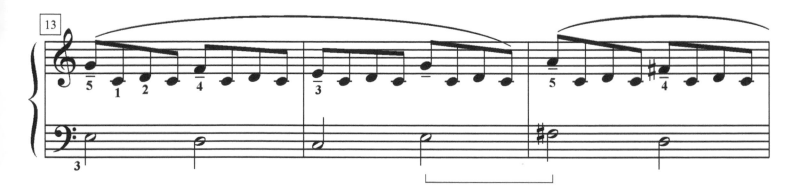

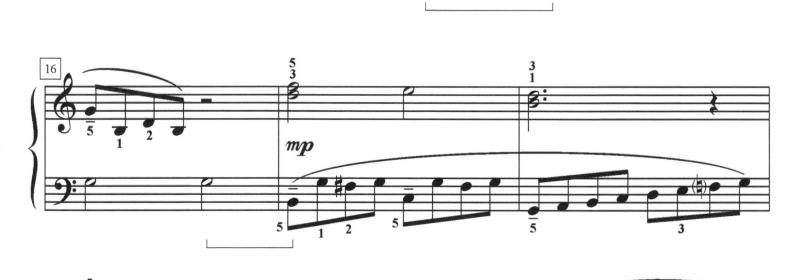

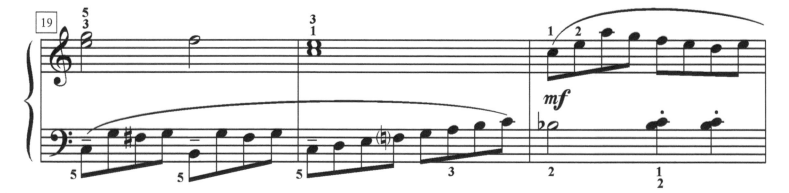

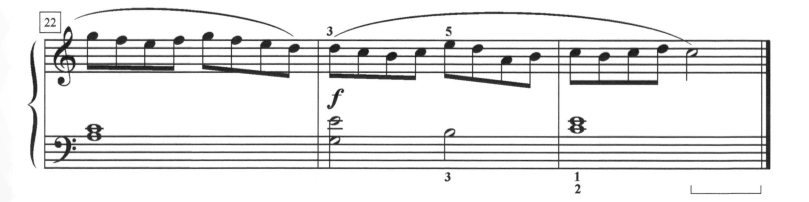

Trill Exercise

Andante ♪ = 100-108

Fritz Spindler, Op. 308, No. 28

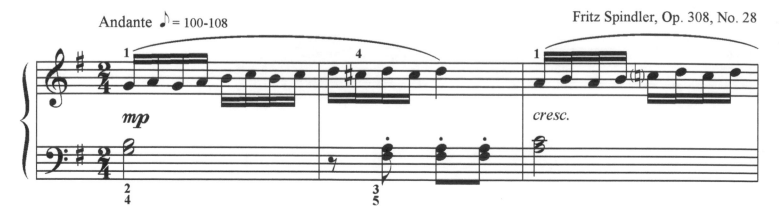

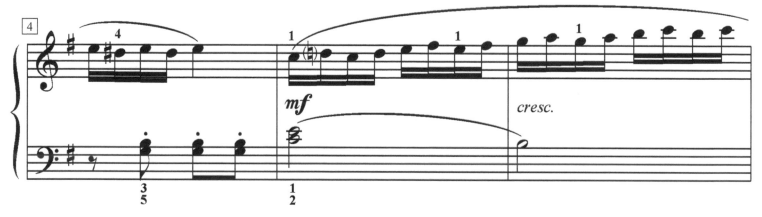

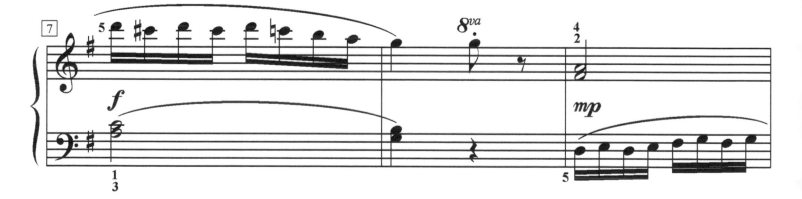

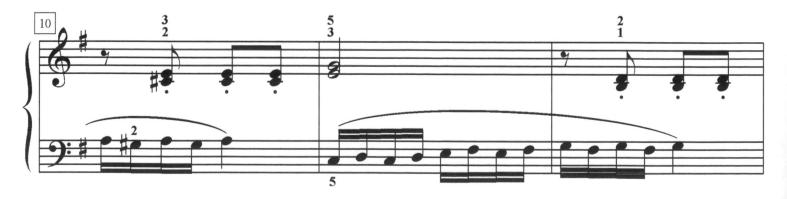

Rotation Etude

Andantino ♩= 96-104

Friedrich Brauer, Op. 15, No. 7

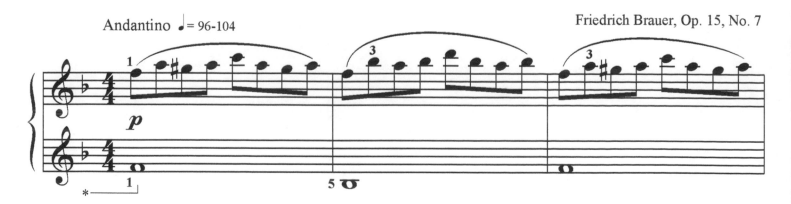

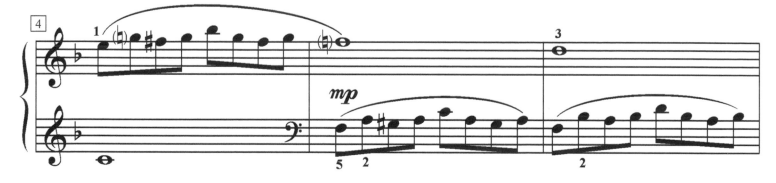

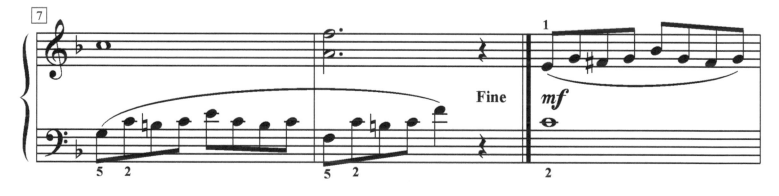

* This pedal mark is used when repeating after the *D.C. al fine*.

Hand Extensions

Cantabile ♩ = 96-104

based on Johann B. Cramer, *50 Studies*, No. 5

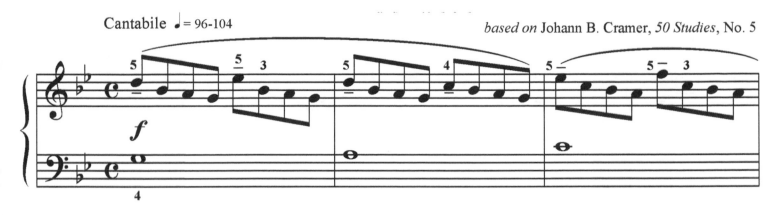

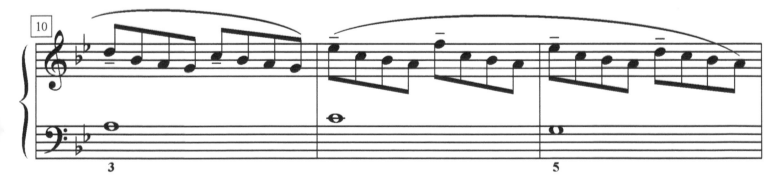

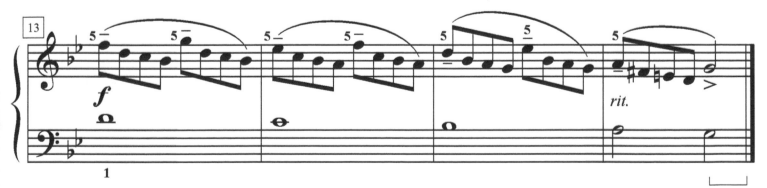

Phrases with Staccato Release

Andante ♩= 88-100

Giuseppe Concone, Op. 24, No. 1

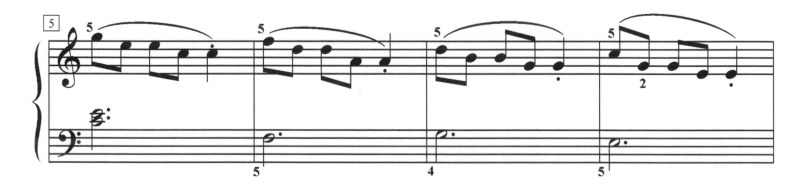

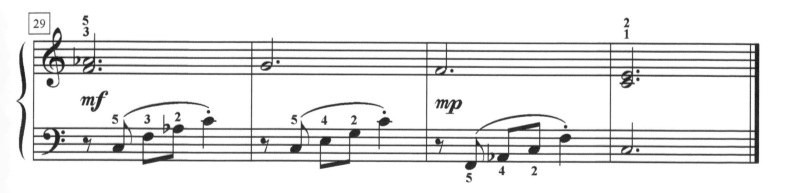

Left Hand Phrase Groups

Carl Czerny, Op. 139, No. 69

C-Minor Study

Espressione ♩= 88-96

Johann B. Cramer, *50 Studies*, No. 7

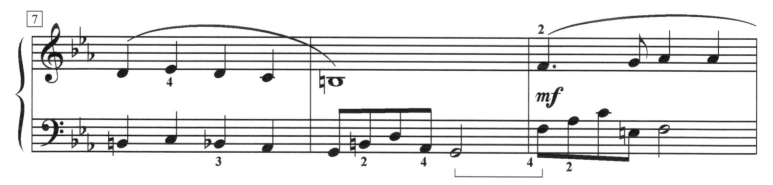